Looking at...
LIFE ON THE STREETS

Kaye Stearman

WAYLAND

First published in 2009 by Wayland

Copyright © Wayland 2009

Wayland
338 Euston Road
London NW1 3BH

Wayland Australia
Level 17/207 Kent Street
Sydney NSW 2000

Produced for Wayland by
White-Thomson Publishing Ltd

+44 (0) 845 362 8240
www.wtpub.co.uk

Editors: Sonya Newland and Katie Powell
Designer: Robert Walster

British Library Cataloguing in Publication Data
Stearman, Kaye
 Looking at life on the streets
 1. Street life - Juvenile literature
 I. Title II. Life on the streets
 307.7'6

ISBN: 9780750259002

Picture Credits

Associated Press: 36, 43; Corbis: *cover* (Ashley Cooper), 12 (Mark Peterson), 37 (Robert Benson); Dreamstime: 31 (Sascha Dunkhorst), 44 bottom (Rmarmion); Eye Ubiquitous: 4 (J. Hulme), 8 (David Cummings), 14 (David Cummings), 16 (Michael George), 20 (Julia Waterlow), 24 (Jason Burke), 26 (Johnstone), 27 (Philip Wolmuth), 29 (Skjold); Format: 38 (Lisa Woollett); Sally and Richard Greenhill Picture Library: 34; Robert Harding: 42 (Jeff Greenberg); Hodder Wayland Picture Library: *title page*, *contents*, 10 bottom, 15 (© Shelter), 17 (Howard Davies), 19 (Martyn Chillmaid), 24, 35, 40, 44 top (J. Holmes), 45 (Zak Waters); Impact: 4 (Peter Arkell); iStock: 6; Panos: 13 (Paul Quayle), 25 (Giacomo Pirozzi), 39 (Giacomo Pirozzi); Popperfoto: 10 top, 11, 15, 32, 33; Rex Features: 21 (Nina Bermann); Chris Schwarz: *contents top*, 5, 9, 18, 22, 27, 28, 30, 33, 41 top and bottom; Roger Vlitos: 7, 22.

Every attempt has been made to clear copyright. Should there be any inadvertent omission please apply to the publisher for rectification.

Printed in China

Wayland is a division of Hachette Children's Books, an Hachette UK company.
www.hachette.co.uk

CONTENTS

Homelessness

Can you imagine what life would be like without a proper home? You would have no bedroom to sleep in, no kitchen for cooking and no bathroom for washing. Now imagine you have hardly any money. How would you manage?

⬆ This girl has made a shelter out of a crate on the streets of London.

Sleeping and eating

You would need to find somewhere to sleep and keep your belongings. Maybe you could sleep on a park bench or in a shop doorway. If you are lucky you might have a sleeping bag or a blanket, but you could be worried that someone might steal them.

You would have to beg people for money or food. You might even have to eat the food that other people throw away.

➡ This young boy has to beg on the streets of Bangkok, Thailand.

Washing

You would need to wash at street taps or in public toilets. Your skin, hair and clothes would soon be dirty. It would be easy to get ill.

'Being homeless can mean having no money, no security, no future.'

SHELTER, HOUSING CHARITY, UK

Surviving on the streets

It would be hard to find a proper job. Perhaps you could be a busker or clean car windows at traffic lights. You might end up begging, or even stealing, to get enough money to survive.

Life might not be bad in the summer, but what about in the winter when you are cold and hungry? How would you manage then?

⬇ Night shelters for homeless people are often overcrowded. This man eats his food in the toilets.

Universal problems

Homeless people come from all different backgrounds. There are children, women and men, young and old people. Each has a different story to tell about their life and different ideas about the world.

Homeless people do share many experiences, though. They often come from families that do not have much money. They may have been in children's homes because of family problems.

'Packing up and unpacking, packing up and unpacking. You'd just get comfortable and Dad would want to move again.'
HOMELESS WOMAN, USA

⬅ This homeless teenage girl sits in a doorway. She has nowhere to go.

CASE STUDY ▸ CASE STUDY ▸ CASE STUDY ▸ CASE STUDY ▸

As a child, Martin never had a proper home. His family was always on the move. They rented houses, flats, even a mobile home. When they finally stopped moving, it was too late for Martin. He couldn't settle. He had never stayed anywhere long enough to make friends or keep up with schooling.

He began skipping school and spending time on the streets with other truants. At first it was great. The group begged and busked on the streets and in shopping malls. Sometimes they stole clothes or DVDs and CDs. Martin was caught stealing and had to go to court. Eventually he ended up in prison.

When Martin left prison, he didn't want to see his family. He couldn't get a job because he had a criminal record. He began drifting into a life on the streets.

➔ Without money, family or friends, homeless people face a bleak future.

A worldwide problem

No one knows exactly how many homeless people there are in the world. Some countries have censuses, where they count the population, but homeless people are often not counted. Many will avoid government officials.

⬆ This family in Calcutta, India, lives and sleeps on the streets. They may stay here for years.

Changing numbers

Another problem is that numbers keep changing. Some people only stay on the streets for a short time and then go home. Others find shelter in a hostel or sleep on a friend's floor. But sometimes the days and weeks on the streets turn into months and years.

Poor countries

The most homeless people are found in developing countries. Many people go to the cities hoping to find work. Some find shelter, but others cannot afford a home near enough to the city.

⬇ Some homeless people have spent years on the road.

Rich countries

There are fewer homeless people in richer countries. But those that do live on the streets are often found in the cities, too.

In richer countries, governments sometimes help people find homes they can afford, especially if they are families or old people. Many homeless people are not able to get government help, though.

Others don't want the government to interfere. They just want to be left alone to manage without help.

FACT

Experts think that there are around 100 million people in the world who don't have a home. This includes people who sleep outside, in public buildings or in temporary night shelters. Just imagine 100 million people – that's twice the population of England.

'AN URBANIZING WORLD', UN CENTRE FOR HUMAN SETTLEMENTS, GENEVA, SWITZERLAND.

Why are people homeless?

People leave their homes for many different reasons. There may have been a disaster such as an earthquake or a flood. People may have fled because their country was at war. Some people leave their homes just because they want to find a better life.

Why do people move to cities?

One of the biggest movements is from the countryside to the cities. Some people go to find work in cities because it is becoming more difficult to make a living from activities such as farming. Other people go to the cities to join family or friends, or because they want the 'buzz' of city life.

⬆ These slums are built over an open sewer in Indonesia.

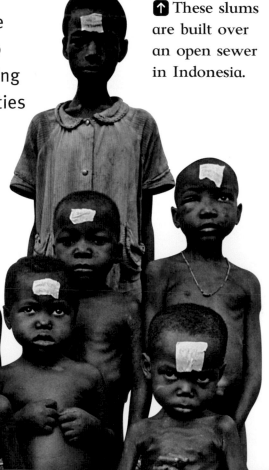

➡ Many African children have lost their homes and families because of wars. These orphans have their names stuck to their heads, so that aid workers can identify them.

FACT

In 2004, 1.8 million people were left homeless after an earthquake beneath the Indian Ocean triggered a tsunami that swept ashore. More than 10 countries were affected. The tsunami washed away whole villages, leaving those who survived with nowhere to live. Aid agencies helped build temporary shelters, and later started planning permanent homes, but, by 2008, thousands of people were still homeless.

⬆ A little girl cuddles her dog among the wreckage of her home, which was destroyed by a hurricane.

The cost of housing

People can have problems when they get to the city, though. Housing costs a lot in cities and many people cannot afford it. Some stay in cheap boarding houses. Others live in shanty towns on the outskirts of cities, where shelters are built from whatever people can find – wood, bricks or plastic sheets.

In the worst cases people find themselves living on the streets. They may build shelters on the pavements. They may sleep in doorways or even in sewers under the city streets.

The true meaning of homelessness

What does it really mean to be without a home? Here are four types of homeless people:

• People without a roof, who sleep rough on the streets, in railway stations, or under bridges.

⬇ This young man has a bed in a night shelter, but he is still homeless.

• People without a house, who sleep in night shelters, hostels or other temporary shelters.

• People in temporary houses, living in empty buildings, in shanty towns or in refugee camps.

• People in houses that lack basic facilities, such as electricity or running water.

For every one homeless person sleeping rough, there are many more who find some form of shelter.

CASE STUDY ► CASE STUDY ► CASE STUDY ► CASE STUDY ►

Anita is 10 years old and comes from Jaipur, a city in Rajasthan, India. She lives in a small hut. The walls are made from old bricks, the roof from tin and plastic sheets and the floor is the pavement. There is no running water or electricity. Anita's family uses the hut to sleep, dress and store their few belongings, and they cook, eat and work on the pavement outside.

Anita's parents left their village years ago. Now they make a living by ironing clothes for wealthier people. Anita collects and delivers the heavy clothing, helps with washing and cooking, and watches the younger children. She does go to school, but she finds it hard to concentrate.

Despite all the problems, Anita's family prefers living in Jaipur to being in the village — at least they can make a living in the city.

➡ This little girl and her family live in a slum in Jaipur, India.

'People come to the city looking for work and a livelihood. They are not looking for a home. They have homes in villages. They leave those homes to look for jobs. So even if their huts are knocked down, they will sleep on pavements.'
ANAND PATWARDHAN, FILM DIRECTOR, INDIA

Poverty and homelessness

The most common reason for homelessness is poverty. Poverty means not having enough money to enjoy a good standard of life, which most people agree should include:

- Good-quality food to stay healthy and active.

- Clean running water for drinking and washing.

- Basic goods such as clothes or furniture.

- Safe housing with room for everyone.

- Healthy neighbourhoods with clean streets.

⬇ Squatters in Calcutta, India, must use public facilities such as this water tank to wash.

Slums in the shadow of skyscrapers in Jakarta, Indonesia.

The cost of homes

Millions of people are too poor to buy or rent a proper home. Some of them do not have jobs at all, but others work for wages. Even if a whole family works, though, they still may not be able to afford proper housing.

Squatters

People who live in empty buildings or on disused land are called 'squatters'. Most squatters have moved into these places without permission, so they have no rights to either the land or the homes they have built.

City councils are often ashamed of squatter settlements. They think the squatters give the city a bad image. Many squatters are forced out, or evicted. Their homes are knocked down and their belongings are destroyed. There is no compensation: people have to find somewhere else to live and start all over again.

Four children share one bed in a damp, cold room in a squat.

The search for shelter

Although there are problems finding work and somewhere to live in the growing cities, people in both developed and developing countries are still moving there from the countryside in search of a better life.

Changing patterns

People's housing needs change as the patterns of their lives change. In developed countries, older

➡ When people leave poor areas for better ones, the poor areas become even more run-down.

FACT

About 600 million city-dwellers in Africa, Asia and Latin America crowd into housing without running water or proper drainage and rubbish collection.

'An Urbanizing World', UN Centre for Human Settlements, Geneva, Switzerland.

industries find that the goods they make can be produced more cheaply elsewhere. Factories close down and jobs are lost. People move away from the area. Because there are fewer people, places like shops and cafés make less money and many close down, and even more people move away. Eventually whole neighbourhoods become run-down or deserted.

➡ Rich and poor houses are often found side-by-side. This is Kingston, the capital of Jamaica.

Rising prices

Houses may not be available in areas where people want to live. After all, who would choose to live in an area where there is heavy pollution or a high crime rate? Most people prefer a safe, friendly neighbourhood. The result is that houses in the most popular areas get more expensive. Some people have to move to cheaper areas, with poorer housing and facilities.

FACT

Each year thousands of people move from northern England to seek jobs in London and the south. As a result, some northern cities have rows of empty houses, while new houses are needed in southern England.

THE GUARDIAN.

No job, no home, no hope?

People move for many reasons – to find work, to go to college or to get married. Others want to leave their past behind and start a new life. Most people do find a new home, even if it is not exactly what they are looking for. Finding a job is often the first step on the long road to finding a good home.

FACT

A survey of homeless people in 30 American cities found that one in five had a job but couldn't afford a room.

NATIONAL COALITION FOR THE HOMELESS.

⬇ High unemployment rates means that lots of people compete for jobs.

CASE STUDY ▸ CASE STUDY ▸ CASE STUDY ▸ CASE STUDY ▸

Tom has been homeless since he left his family in the north of England six months ago. He couldn't find a job locally, so he hitched a ride to London and stayed with friends. He found work with a fast-food chain but couldn't find a room nearby that he could afford. He joined a group squatting in an empty house, but they were evicted after a few months. Tom went back to sleeping on people's floors, but there were always problems such as fights and drugs. He was so tired he was always late for work and got fired.

Tom wants to work and he wants somewhere to live. But it is difficult to find and keep a job without a proper place to live. And without a job, he can't afford somewhere to live. He feels trapped.

➡ A homeless youth looking for work. Even a low-paid job may not be enough to pay for a room.

The right place

However, there are other people who end up on the streets because they cannot find a home that is suitable. They may not be able to find something of the right size or with the right facilities. They may find there is nothing available in the area they want to live at a price they can afford.

The housing problem

In some places there is enough housing for everyone, but some of it remains empty. This is often because the houses are too expensive. The most expensive housing is found in rich cities such as New York, London and Paris. But even outside these areas, houses are too expensive for many people.

Land use

In many countries, governments limit the amount of land that can be used for housing. Because there is not much land, it becomes even more expensive. Also, the land is divided into smaller and smaller parcels, and houses and flats become smaller.

⬆ High-rise blocks in Hong Kong. This kind of housing is common in big cities.

'Poor people find it difficult to pay for housing, food, child care and education. Housing often takes the largest proportion of people's income. Being poor means being an illness, an accident or a paycheck away from living on the streets.'
NATIONAL COALITION FOR THE HOMELESS, USA

Discrimination

Another problem is discrimination. The people who own or rent houses (landlords) may prefer single people to families, for example. Or they may prefer local people to foreigners, or white people to black people. People with disabilities, or families with small children, often find it hard to get suitable housing.

Many countries now have laws saying that it is wrong to treat people in this way, but discrimination still happens. Most people do not want to live somewhere they feel unwanted. They prefer to live somewhere more friendly, even if this means they pay higher prices for housing.

➡ This man has lost his job and his home and must beg on the streets of Washington, D.C., USA.

Living on the streets

Life on the streets can be unpredictable, but this does not mean that street people live in chaos. In fact, most homeless people try to develop a daily routine.

This is not always possible, though, especially if people are forced to keep moving by police and other authorities. We met Anita and Martin on pages 13 and 17. Here is a breakdown of their days:

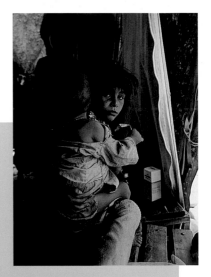

⬇ This Indian girl spends a lot of time looking after younger brothers and sisters.

Anita's day

05.15	Wakes up
05.30	Fetches milk
05.45	Sweeps pavement around hut
06.00	Fetches clothes for ironing from customers
07.00	Has bath and breakfast
07.30	Leaves for school
13.15	Returns from school, has leftovers for lunch
13.30	Delivers bundles of ironed clothes to customers
15.00	Sweeps and cleans, does homework
16.00	Fetches milk
16.30	More deliveries to customers
21.00	Deliveries finally finished, dozes off exhausted
22.30	Woken to eat with parents
23.00	Sleeps, sharing rope bed with two younger sisters

Martin's day

05.00 Wakes up on pavement, as streets cleaners approach
05.15 Packs belongings, buys coffee from stall
06.00 Walks around, talks with other homeless people
07.30 Sits outside station begging from travellers, moved on by police
09.30 Buys breakfast, washes at public toilets
10.30 Walks across city in search of work — no luck
13.15 Begs from shoppers in mall, moved on by security guards
14.30 Finds half-eaten sandwich in bin, falls asleep in park
16.00 Attends drop-in clinic for treatment of old injury
17.30 Queues for hostel bed but hostel is full
19.30 Beds down on pavement
21.30 Wakes up, talks and drinks with other homeless people
24.00 Bread and soup delivered by charity
01.00 Drifts back to sleep on pavement

Daily routines

People in different circumstances have different routines, but they still have to do all the everyday things that other people do. Anita, who lives with her family on the pavement in India, and Martin, who sleeps rough in a big American city, both have to eat, sleep and wash, for example.

➡ These men are used to eating and sleeping in doorways.

Strength in numbers

Some homeless people band together to keep themselves safe. They may share food, drink or drugs. They may watch out for each other or try to protect weaker people from being beaten up. Because children are smaller and weaker than adults, and are easier to bully, they are more likely to hang around in groups.

⬇ These children from Rio de Janeiro in Brazil are poor but have a home to go to.

Other homeless people are loners, preferring to rely on their own skills to keep them safe on the streets.

⬅ Many homeless people spend their days in parks, bus stops and other public places.

CASE STUDY ▸ CASE STUDY ▸ CASE STUDY ▸ CASE STUDY ▸

Bekele lives on the streets of Addis Ababa, the capital of Ethiopia. He is 11 years old and has been homeless since his mother died two years ago. At first he was alone but now he belongs to a gang of other young boys who look out for each other.

The boys hang around the same area. They share the leftover food they get from hotels. They run errands, carry goods and look after parked cars. Sometimes they beg or steal. The older children try to protect the young ones and do their best to help those who are ill or injured. They fear being caught by shopkeepers or police, who often beat and imprison them.

Bekele is one of millions of homeless children around the world. Most live on the city streets of Asia, Africa and Latin America, but there are also homeless children in richer countries. These children are often described as 'street children', although many do stay in touch with their families. Street children spend their days – and often their nights – on the streets.

➡ Street children sleeping rough in Kigali, Rwanda.

Money matters

Homeless people find many ways to get money. In poor countries, most homeless people work, but often their jobs are the most dirty and difficult. They may work on building sites, collect and recycle rubbish, or fetch and carry goods. This work is usually poorly paid, so it is hard for people to earn enough to buy or rent a home.

⬆ It can be hard to find work if you are alone with a baby to care for, too.

Child workers

In many countries, poor children earn money by providing some sort of service. They may run errands, carry shopping, shine shoes or sort rubbish. Some search the streets for bottles or cardboard that they can sell. Some children beg or steal, either on their own or as part of a gang.

➡ These women in South Africa earn money by making bricks.

Work in wealthy countries

It is harder to find work such as carrying shopping or sorting rubbish in richer countries. People have cars to transport their shopping, and rubbish collection and recycling is done by machines. Many regular jobs require a good education or special skills. As a result, many homeless people have to beg from passers-by or depend on charity. Some earn money by busking – playing music or singing. Some find odd jobs or get rewarded for small services.

⬆ Busking on the streets is one way to earn money. This boy plays for onlookers in Krakow, Poland.

'They just don't want to work.'
PASSER-BY, SYDNEY, AUSTRALIA

'I'd like to work, but who will employ someone like me?'
HOMELESS PERSON, NEW YORK, USA

Health and safety

The chances are that you will still be alive when you are 70 or even 80, and so will most of your friends. But a person living on the streets is not so lucky. Their health is so badly affected by living rough that most of them die before they are 45 or 50.

The risks of street life

People who live on the streets are outside in even the worst weather. They eat bad food and it is hard to keep clean, so they are more likely to catch diseases. They might be attacked at night while sleeping outside.

'I'd rather die on the streets than in hospital.'
HOMELESS MAN, PARIS, FRANCE

'Would you want to sit in a doctor's waiting room next to a dirty street person?'
NURSE WORKING WITH HOMELESS MEN, GLASGOW, SCOTLAND

➡ A rare chance to seek medical help at this drop-in clinic for homeless people in Moscow, Russia.

CASE STUDY ▸ CASE STUDY ▸ CASE STUDY ▸ CASE STUDY ▸

Mike has lived on the streets for years. He is in his thirties but looks much older. Although he is tough, he is actually very ill. He coughs a lot and his skin is covered with sores.

Mike is sick because he eats left-over food from rubbish bins. He catches diseases when he sleeps in crowded shelters. Although Mike tries to keep clean and dry, it is hard without running water and proper shelter.

Mike knows that he is ill but he doesn't want to go to the hospital. He doesn't trust doctors or nurses. In any case, he has no money to pay for medicines or a quiet place to recover.

Getting help

It can be hard to get medical treatment. Street people often have special problems, like lung diseases or bad feet. They may be afraid to go to a hospital, or too poor to pay for medical help.

⬆ A homeless man tries to sleep on a park bench on a cold winter's day.

Drink and drugs

Some homeless people have problems with alcohol or drugs. They might inject heroin, sniff glue or become addicted to gambling. An addict is a person who has a desperate need for a substance or activity. People can be cured of addictions, but treatment is nearly always long and expensive.

⬇ Some homeless people are addicted to alcohol or drugs. Without help, it is difficult to overcome their addiction.

Addiction leads to homelessness

Some people may spend everything on their addiction, and then find they cannot pay their rent. Others leave home after family arguments, especially if they have

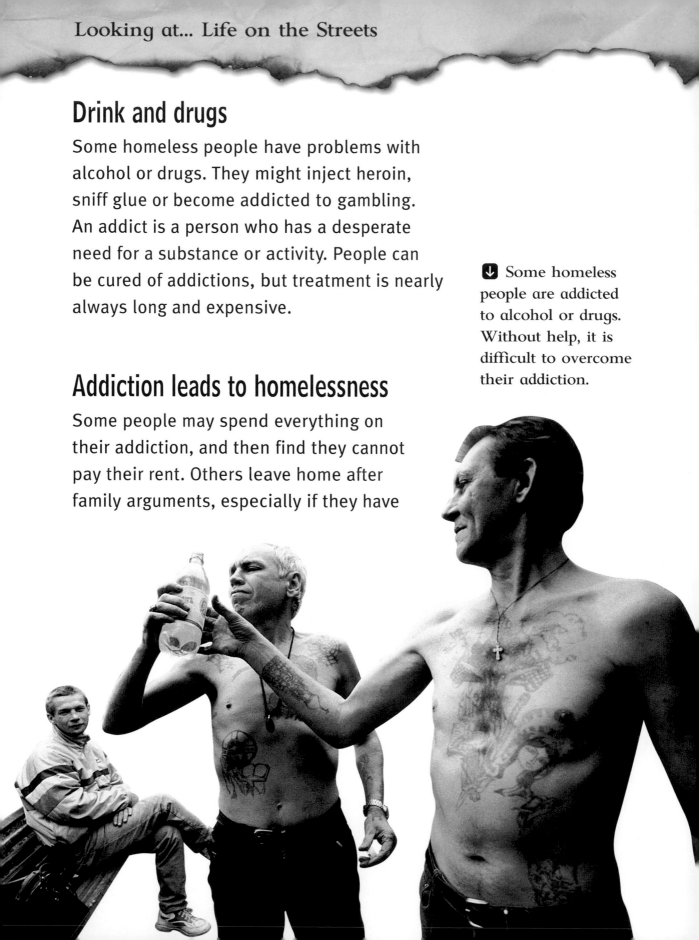

← This homeless man is forced to beg. Alone on the streets, he faces many dangers.

'I don't blame people for walking past. I suppose they think I'm already dead.'
HOMELESS MAN, LONDON

been stealing to pay for their addiction. Once on the streets, they may find that the only way to survive is to turn to crime.

Addicts on the streets

People may also become addicted after they become homeless. Drinking alcohol or taking drugs may help them to cope with day-to-day life on the streets. A cold night or an empty stomach might be warmed by alcohol or sniffing glue. And, if the people around you drink or take drugs, it is easy to fall into the same habits.

FACT

Most homeless people are not addicts. Some may drink alcohol or take drugs but they do not become addicts. Alcohol or drugs are only a small part of their problems. However, many homeless people are in bad health or have mental illness.

SHELTER,
HOUSING CHARITY.

Street-life dangers

Here are a few of the things that can make street life difficult and dangerous:

- Going hungry and eating poor-quality food.

- Drinking too much alcohol.

- Sharing dirty needles when taking drugs.

- Being pushed into criminal activities.

- Being robbed or losing your few possessions.

- Being arrested or moved on by the police.

- Being attacked and beaten.

- Being run down by cars.

- Being evicted from squats or pavement shelters.

FACT

Homeless people feel threatened by other members of the street community and by the general public, too.

SHELTER,
HOUSING CHARITY

➡ This Filippino family have no home and have to eat in unclean places, but they have each other for support.

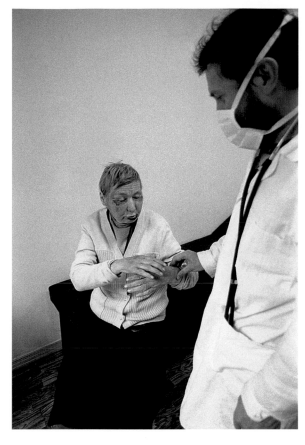

'People tell me to get off the streets and go to a night shelter. Night shelters are dirty and dangerous. You are more likely to get robbed in a shelter than on the street. I prefer to take my chances outside.'
HOMELESS MAN, NEW YORK

← Beaten and bruised, this woman has fled a violent home. But can she find somewhere safe to go?

Women and children

Children are most at risk on the streets. In some countries, gangs and police have attacked and killed street children. Some have been picked up by criminals who force them to sell their bodies or push them into crime.

Homeless women, and their children, are also at particular risk. Many women leave their homes to escape violence. They often find themselves without support, and have to live on the streets, in hostels, shelters or squats.

↑ A homeless woman in the Philippines. All her belongings are on the pavement after she has been turned out of her squatter home.

Supporting street people

Most homeless people don't want to be on the streets – they would like a proper home like everyone else. However, they face huge difficulties, including finding somewhere they can afford and overcoming the prejudices that other people have against street people.

Facing fears

Many homeless people are frightened, and feel that they cannot cope with the responsibility of looking after a home. They may have escaped from a violent home, only to face further violence on the streets.

⬇ Support from the staff at a drop-in centre can be the first step towards a life away from the streets.

Often homeless people feel that they are worthless. The biggest challenge they must overcome is learning to believe in themselves, to feel that they can cope with a settled life away from the life they know on the streets.

Moving off the streets

A gradual, step-by-step approach is often the only way to get people off the streets. Groups that work with homeless people first try to gain their trust. They may encourage them to visit a drop-in centre or talk with a doctor or nurse. They may persuade people to use night shelters or hostels. This can encourage people to start thinking about finding permanent housing.

⬆ A street kitchen to feed homeless people, run by a charity.

Not everyone wants to leave the streets. Some find street life interesting. Others prefer it to living in a violent or unhappy home.

➡ Some people are so used to a life outside that they don't want to change their ways.

Additional support

Even when people have found a home, they may still need support to stay off the streets. Settling down can be very strange, particularly if it is in an unfamiliar neighbourhood. The local council or a charity might help by offering low-rent housing and help with heating bills, or perhaps bedding and furniture.

'Giving people a place to live is only the start. They need extra help. One man panicked every time he got a bill. We had to explain them and show him how to pay. Other people had to learn how to shop or cook.'

WORKER SUPPORTING HOMELESS PEOPLE, SHEFFIELD, UK

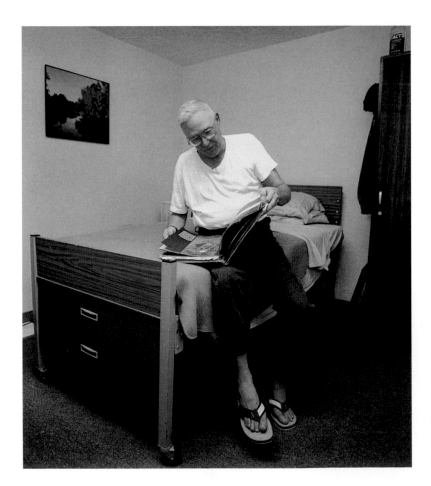

← This man fought in the Vietnam War, and then spent years on the streets. Now he has a room provided for him by a special charity.

CASE STUDY ▸ CASE STUDY ▸ CASE STUDY ▸ CASE STUDY ▸

Marie was overjoyed when she finally got her own flat. Ever since she had left home years before, she had wanted somewhere to call her own. She had been in and out of children's homes, temporary hostels and bed-and-breakfast hotels. Now she had her own flat and her own tiny baby.

But life was much more difficult than she imagined. Her new flat had hardly any furniture and it was often cold. She had to find money for rent, heating and electricity as well as food and clothes. She wasn't used to cooking meals or paying bills and the baby wouldn't stop crying.

But the worst thing was the loneliness. She felt cooped up all day. She had left all her old friends behind. When she was homeless she had often been cold and frightened, but she had never been so lonely.

➡ A young single mother cuddles her baby. Everyone wants to give their children a good start in life.

Getting ready to work

Finding work can be hard. Lots of homeless people have dropped out of school and do not have the skills needed for many jobs. Even when work is available, it is likely to be badly paid and insecure.

There are special schemes to help street people find work. Sometimes they get together to help themselves by selling street papers. They buy papers and then sell them on for a higher price. This can be the first step towards a life off the streets.

⬇ Selling the *Big Issue* on the city streets can teach homeless people skills such as dealing with money.

'We wanted to help homeless people find work. If you are homeless and need a job, you need a place to wash, clean clothes and somewhere to store your belongings. So we called our group SHWASHLOCK – SHowers, WASHers and LOCKers.'

HOMELESS WOMAN, CALIFORNIA

Learning new skills

Selling street papers can help homeless people discover new skills, such as handling money and mixing with other people. Street papers also show the general public that homeless people are willing to help themselves.

⬆ A street child in Cape Verde, West Africa, learning carpentry. This skill may help him to a life off the streets.

Helping street children

Many countries have schemes to help street children. There are drop-in centres where children can learn lessons and skills to earn money. This gives them a better chance of getting away from the dangers of street life.

FACT

Street News, the world's first street paper, started in New York city in 1989. A year later *the Big Issue* appeared in London. Now there are more than 100 street papers worldwide.

THE BIG ISSUE, LONDON, UK.

Looking for solutions

Homelessness has been a problem for hundreds of years. For example, in sixteenth-century England, one in four people were 'roaming vagabonds' – people without land or homes. In America in the 1930s, millions of poor farmers lost their farms because of drought.

Rising numbers of homeless

You might think that as countries get richer, there would be fewer people living on the streets, but this is not always the case. In some countries, there are more homeless people now than at any other point in history. Although living conditions are improving for many people, the very poorest people still live in very difficult conditions.

⬆ Even many years ago, groups of poor children lived and worked on the city streets.

'Only five per cent of people sleeping rough do so from choice. The most common reason is the breakdown of relations with parents or a partner. Between one quarter and one third of rough sleepers have been in children's homes or foster care.'

REPORT OF THE SOCIAL EXCLUSION UNIT, UK GOVERNMENT

Facts about street people:

- Most homeless people are from poor families.

- Many dropped out of school or lack job skills.

- Many young people have been in children's homes or in foster care.

- Many have been in prison.

- Some are homeless because they are mentally ill or have addictions.

- Many homeless people could find a home if cheaper housing was available.

⬆ Many homeless people have spent time in prison.

⬇ A homeless man has a cup of tea and a quiet nap in a night café.

Helping the homeless

There are many ways in which governments and charities try to help people living on the streets. They provide money and food, medical care and legal advice. These efforts help many people, but they don't tackle the reasons that people become homeless in the first place.

Preventing homelessness

Homelessness is a bit like a revolving door – as soon as one person goes out another comes in. It is important to find ways of dealing with the situations that force people to live on the streets.

Most people cope on a day-to-day basis. But coping in a crisis, when everything seems to happen at once, can be much more difficult. Often, at the worst times, the support people need isn't available.

⬇ Volunteers at a drop-in centre for the homeless serve food to those who need it.

Finding solutions

How can we help people in these situations? Sometimes the answer might be more money, but it might be other things, too, such as providing education, job training, treatment for addictions, support for broken families and cheaper housing. Often the needs of homeless people are so big that only government action can make a difference.

⬆ Nowhere else to go. A homeless man protests against a city law that bans homeless people from sleeping on city pavements in Detroit, USA.

'We managed okay with mortgage payments. Then I lost my job. We couldn't afford the mortgage any more and ended up losing our house.'
HOMELESS MAN, MANCHESTER, UK

'After my wife died, I just couldn't cope. I cut myself off from everyone and started drinking. I ended up on the streets.'
HOMELESS MAN, NEW YORK, USA

'After my mum remarried I just couldn't get on with my new stepdad. I ran away from home and started sleeping on people's floors.'
HOMELESS TEENAGER, SYDNEY, AUSTRALIA

Homes great and small

People's homes come in many different types and sizes. Some are large and many are very small. Some families have two homes. Others have to share one or two rooms in run-down buildings. Some people sleep on the streets.

Ending homelessness

Do we end homelessness by building more homes or sharing what we have more fairly? Do we help people after they become homeless, or do we try to stop them becoming homeless in the first place? What do you think?

⬆ This Chinese father and son are proud of their flat. It may be small but it is clean and well-maintained.

⬅ This family is moving into a comfortable home, with plenty of room and space to play.

CASE STUDY ▶ CASE STUDY ▶

More than anything, Nina wants her own bedroom. She hates sharing with her sisters. Her older sister guards her space fiercely and warns Nina not to touch her things. Her little sister makes such a mess that Nina is always tidying up after her.

Some of Nina's friends have their own rooms. One even has a separate playroom. 'Lucky thing,' thinks Nina. 'My own room, decorated the way I want – that would be bliss.'

But Nina knows that things could be much worse. Some of her school friends share rooms with three or more people. Their families can't afford a bigger place.

She also knows two girls who live in hotels. Nina thought it sounded great until she discovered that these were special hotels for homeless families. Each family lives and sleeps in one room and has to queue to use one kitchen. There is no room to play and the girls can't invite friends round. Nina's mum says that in some countries tiny children live on the streets, without proper homes or families. She says Nina should be grateful she only shares with her sisters.

⬆ Sharing a room, even when you get on well together, can sometimes be a strain.

GLOSSARY

Addiction

When a person has a desperate need for something, such as alcohol or drugs, and cannot give it up without help.

Bed-and-breakfast

Temporary housing – often residents have to leave each morning and spend their days on the streets.

Busking

Entertainment performed in the street for passers-by. Buskers might sing or play a musical instrument.

Census

When the government tries to count every person living in a particular country.

Charity

A group that aims to help people or provide something without making a profit.

Compensation

A payment to make up for loss or damage.

Discrimination

Treating people differently and unfairly, often because of their colour or sex.

Drop-in centre

Services that people can use without an appointment.

Eviction

An order by a landlord or council to leave an area or a building/home.

Heroin

A very addictive drug made from morphine that is usually injected by users.

Hostel

Temporary accommodation, normally sharing rooms with other people.

Landlord

Property owner. Can be a person, a company, a charity or a government agency.

Mental illness

Sickness of the mind, sometimes caused by stress, alcohol or drugs.

Mortgage

A loan given to buy a property, usually paid off over a long period of time.

Night shelter

Temporary bed and facilities for homeless people (often run by charities).

Recycle

Collect and convert waste for new uses.

Refugee

Someone who flees their country to escape persecution.

Rent

Payments to a landlord for use of a property.

Rough sleeper

A person who sleeps in the open – usually on the streets.

Shanty towns

Areas where people live in temporary shelters, built from whatever they can find, often on the outskirts of cities in developing countries.

Squat

To occupy an empty or unused building or land without the permission of the owner.

Squatter settlements

Makeshift homes constructed on empty, unused or waste land, often against the law.

FURTHER INFORMATION

ORGANIZATIONS

Worldwide, there are many organizations working to end homelessness. The organizations below can provide more information.

Australia

The Council to Homeless Persons
2 Stanley Street
Collingwood
Victoria 3066
Tel: (03) 9419 8699
www.chp.org.au

Canada

National Anti-Poverty Organization
1 Nicholas Street, Suite 1210
Ottawa
Ontario K1N 7B7
Tel: (613) 789 0096
http://english.napo-onap.ca

Ireland

Focus Ireland
9–12 High Street
Christchurch
Dublin 8
Tel: (01) 881 5900
www.focusireland.ie

UK

Homeless International
Queens House
16 Queens Road
Coventry CV1 3EG
Tel: (024) 7663 2802
www.homeless-international.org

Shelter (England)
88 Old Street
London EC1V 9HU
Helpline: 0808 800 4444
http://england.shelter.org.uk

Shelter (Wales)
25 Walter Road
Swansea SA1 1ZZ
www.sheltercymru.org.uk

Shelter (Northern Ireland)
165 University Street
Belfast BT17 1HR
http://northernireland.shelter.org.uk

Shelter (Scotland)
4th floor, Scotiabank House
6 South Charlotte Street
Edinburgh EH2 4AW
http://scotland.shelter.org.uk

Y Care International
Kemp House
152–160 City Road
London EC1V 2NP
Tel: 020 7549 3150
www.ycareinternational.org

USA

National Coalition for the Homeless
1012 Fourteenth Street NW #600
Washington DC 20005-3410 USA
Tel:
www.nationalhomeless.org

FURTHER READING

It Happened to Me: Runaway
by A. Neustatter and H. Elliott
(Franklin Watts, 2003)

Living as a Refugee (Real Life Stories)
(Ticktock Media, 2005)

Street Life (Real Life Stories)
(Ticktock Media, 2005)

Talk About: Homelessness
by Kaye Stearman
(Wayland, 2008)

Working with Homeless People
by Diane Church
(Franklin Watts, 2001)

INDEX